Fun A

by Steve Munson

HOUGHTON MIFFLIN BOSTON

PHOTOGRAPHY CREDITS: Cover © Blend Images/Veer; Toc © Comstock Images/Jupiter Images; 2-3 © Blend Images/Veer; 4 © Comstock Images/Jupiter Images; 5 © dejanristovski/Shutterstock; 6 © Digital Vision Photography/Veer

Printed in China

ISBN-13: 978-0-547-01825-6
ISBN-10: 0-547-01825-8

14 15 16 17 0940 19 18 17 16
4500569761

January

I like to skate.

March

I like to run.

May

I like to jump.

August

I like to swim.

September

I like to read.

Responding

TARGET SKILL Compare and Contrast What is something you like to do in the summer? What is something you like to do in the winter? How are they the same? How are they different?

Write About It

Text to Self Draw a picture of you and your friends having fun in the summer. Write a sentence about your picture.

WORDS TO KNOW

come	**me**

TARGET SKILL **Compare and Contrast** Tell how two things are alike or not.

TARGET STRATEGY **Question** Ask questions about what you are reading.

GENRE **Informational text** gives facts about a topic.